Mountains
and the
Sea

Mountains
and the
Sea

poems by
Brian Glaser

SHANTI ARTS PUBLISHING

BRUNSWICK, MAINE

Published by Shanti Arts Publishing

Interior and cover design by Shanti Arts Designs

Shanti Arts LLC
193 Hillside Road
Brunswick, Maine 04011
shantiarts.com

Cover image by slava-stupachenko / unsplash.com

Printed in the United States of America

ISBN: 978-1-962082-80-8 (softcover)

Library of Congress Control Number: 2025943500

CONTENTS

EARLY POEMS

Me waiting until I was nearly fifty
To credit marvels. Like the tree-clock of tin cans
The tinkers made. So long for air to brighten,
Time to be dazzled and the heart to lighten.

—Seamus Heaney, "Fosterling"

NEW YEAR

This is from the first section of Heinrich Heine's *Deutschland, A Winter's Tale* (1844). Heine was a Jewish poet born in Duesseldorf, a late Romantic émigré to Paris whose eagerness to be assimilated into the *Leitkultur* of his homeland led Theodor Adorno to call him "Heine the Wound."

A new song, a better song—
With flutes and violins.
Ditch the *Miserere*.
It's the dirge that's dead.

Young Europe is in love
With handsome Freedom,
Her genius—arm in arm—
They can't stop kissing.

And though no priest weds them,
Their marriage is true—
Beautiful bride and groom,
And their children, the future.

My song is a wedding song.
The better, the new!
In my soul the stars
Sing their consecration.

Inspired stars, wild and bright
In an avenue of fire—
I feel myself miraculously strong.
I could best an oak.

Since I set feet on German soil
Magic runs in my veins.
The giant has found Mother Earth.
A new strength grows with him.

THE SEA

1.

Looking at Louis Komjathy's magnificent translation of the *Daode Jing*, I find in his notes something initially subtly unsettling, but it becomes quite deep, the channel of thought. He says the text was not written by its legendary purported author, Laozi. Instead, he says, it is the work of centuries of anonymous masters of inner cultivation.

What if we are all anonymous masters—what if that is my fate? What am I the anonymous master of—what vast good will outlive me?

2.

For many years I regretted that I had lived through twenty years of education and never had as a teacher a woman of color. At times this was an intense regret, a scotoma.

Then just last week I remembered that my first American Literature professor in college was of indigenous descent. So I bought her book, published the year after I took her course thirty years ago.

It is pretty dry. And truth be told that is how I found her lectures. Waking in the cold dawns of my first Berkeley fall, walking a full half hour from my dorm to the lecture hall, listening to her talk about autobiographies—Ben Franklin, Harriet Jacobs. It seemed to me that Americans were obsessed by themselves. There was indeed a lot about myself in those days I didn't wish to consider.

3.

Thought while reading Simone Weil: at what point does a philosopher become a systematic philosopher?—A term, usually of disparagement, for thinkers like Hegel and Spinoza. Weil is a liminal case.

Perhaps one becomes a systematic philosopher, unlike William James or Zhuangzi, when one identifies with the human imagination, and so domesticates its essential wildness and sees its energy only inside the system one has created on paper.

4.

Reading about China's Cultural Revolution—the Red Guards
who fomented it were out of control. And the interests of the
leaders, not only Mao, were various, pulling them in many
directions. This without considering the global situation that
played its roles too: imperialism, American and Russian;
other anticapitalisms.

The enormity of the forces beyond the control of any person,
even the authoritarian head of the nation. Above all history
should teach us compassion, compassion for the swimmer in
an indifferent sea. Each moving toward a different land.

ELITISM

—for JL

We all want to be beautiful:
it's a cold wind.

Hovering bird,
who do you love?

Complexity is good,--
a friend who loves your complexity
is better than a god.

It's haunting,
stronger together—

tell it to
the Köln Cathedral,—

stronger together,

the fallen stones,

those simple people
who catch them.

CAPITALISM AND CHRISTIANITY

1.

The fear of the devil, the fear of hell—
going somewhere awful you deserve:
that's the capitalist message to the poor,
the homeless, the proles.

You had your chance,
you didn't make it.

2.

I love to work, too.

Why do I love to work?
My father did.

He could not save me from my teachers,
who assumed all time spent working
was time well spent—

God spent his love on Christ.

GARAGE SAILING

My fifteen-year-old son and I tested the rain
this Saturday morning.

There were two garage sales in our neighborhood
and a handful in the tonier one
on the other side of the freeway.

He found some shirts at the first one,
then nothing for a few tries,
and then a boomerang for three dollars.

He was so excited.

There is a controversy about what drives migration
from the Latin nations to the United States—

my brother-in-law, who owns a chain of appliance stores
in Guatemala,
has a very simple explanation: poverty.

He finds it offensive that the question is being asked
when the answer is so obvious.

And the solution to the problem is free trade.

There is something to this—
the simple enjoyment of trading among neighbors,
the energy with which they appraise another's jewelry,

the eleven-year-old girl
with braided hair who couldn't decide
which of the neighbor's Barbies she needs to take home.

After our sailing
we stopped at the park to learn to throw the boomerang.

The rain was drizzling
and there was a homeless man and his bike
in the small public bathroom.

The boomerang got caught three times in a tree—
each time my son figured out a way to get it down,

climbing into a stout fir tree on the third time,
reaching out onto a slender branch that
I didn't think would bear his weight,

but it did,—
he made it back to *terra firma* safely,

the boomerang and its three-dollar sticker
still belong to us,

and that makes us both happy,
though for two quite different reasons.

SUNDAY AFTERNOON

Throwing the boomerang again today.

My son worked on his form,
throwing against the wind,
finding the right launch angle.

This was at the park where I played at his age,
thirty-five years ago.

The sun was hidden behind a low gray blanket of clouds.

A homeless man shouted at himself
on the basketball court.
A security guard drove by and got out of his car.

After a while,
I sat on the benches beside the baseball diamond
where my son seemed to me perfectly happy
in the outfield.

Though I do not always do it well,
this is what I was made for,
being a father.

How the grass grows in the outfield
of this quiet provincial park

on an overcast Sunday afternoon
before the return of spring,
when an exhausted winter in its solitude offers us nothing.

From the four rows of green painted benches
I sent up a silent shout of gratitude,

amen—

and there you are,
you heard me.

ON A SILENCE

First: do no harm.
Untouched,
like a kelson.

Technology waits
for its shadow.

Would you say:
silences pool?
or, long silences pool?

Kiss the bride,—
there is no game
like water.

Ice and cash:
You decide.

I'll wait for you
beneath the border.

THE ENGLISH MOUNTAIN

Recently I heard a comedian
getting laughs at the expense of the English major:

my friend is eighty thousand bucks in debt
for an English major,

he said,

and he doesn't speak English any better than I do;
I understand every word he says.

The only thing you can do with an English major
is teach English, he said.
It's a pyramid scheme, he said, as the laughter subsided.

A cynic is a man who knows the price of everything
and the value of nothing:
so says Oscar Wilde.

I loved Wilde in college.
All art is quite useless, he said, too.

Wit and inwit:
can you tell them apart?

Market forces.
How will we teach English in twenty years?

I think of my son,
just diagnosed this year with dyslexia—

so much of what my teachers valued about English
would be lost on him—
etymologies, the history of the language—

What will market forces do to a young man in California
who cannot spell?

The more obdurate the scholar,
the safer he is from market forces:

the stone,
in flight:

the union of stones,

toward the history of stones
I throw nothing.

THE SHADOW OF CHARITY

There is a mirror at the edge of a creek
that runs across the first river.

The ice can bear the weight
of a man and a child.

Your steps do
not lead to your dreams.

You let it past you.
It is already gone in the halo of an eye.

My judgment is like water—
I give in the age of looking.

The still, small voice
of joy tells me I am right to do so.

Why should the sky be blue?—
its name is a sign broken open.

ON BEING TERRORIZED

Well,
my best gay student wasn't.

But spies will do anything—
they are like professors in that way—

and most world leaders are psychopaths.

He was nineteen,
and I told him I admired in his poem how he seemed free
to speak his mind wholly,

and he said,
yes, it took me many years to get here.

AFTERNOON CALLING

Whoever you are,
wherever you are on life's journey,
you are welcome here.

I saw this on a church's digital sign
walking home
from wheeling my mother back to the nursing home
with my children on Mother's Day.

I thought:
yes, I am welcome here.

We are welcome here, too.
What a joy.

Thank you,
language, *die Sprache*—

thank you,
all the mediocre
and harmful English teachers I had
who loved themselves unconditionally,
just as they should.

URBAN ORB

Two wood standards
        for a sapling on the sidewalk—
   growing; growing up—

SON AND HEIR

Moving my mother's belongings from her home
to sell it as she
survives in memory care—

my older son spends two afternoons
wrapping and boxing her china—

like the credenza that held it,
a wedding gift of her own china to my parents
from my father's mother,

who grew up in a German ghetto in Cincinnati
and didn't get an education past
sixth grade—

my sister and I can't bear to give it away,
though neither of us wants it—

what an investment for two working class
German Catholics in the Great Depression—

a full set of china—
a month's pay, probably—
to host whom?

My son likes to be told what to do,
home from his first year of college—

he says sometimes he wishes he were
more creative,
like his mother and dad—

he liked wrapping the china,
carefully, with abundant news-wrap
and in boxes he assembled—

maybe,
yes, I will say it:

the point of the china was just that:
it would be carefully wrapped three generations later,

thousands of miles away,—
by a great grandson who likes to be told
what to do—

so I have survived my purpose, too—

henceforth, may it be, money shall pass through me
like a cat through a fence—

SCHOLAR OF THE GREEN WORLD

The
opposite

of
nothing

is
two.

DESIDERATA

I am sitting in the living room
watching the light fade
through the curtains on the longest day
of the year:

letters from friends arrived today,
and my older son
has been cooking peach and tomato bread salad
and lentils with root vegetables, cumin and turmeric:

the light is still here;
I have long been drawn to teachers with extreme views,
though I myself am
in twilight, at midnight—a whole heart, waiting.

MUSIC AS SILENCE

Thinking of my father, who loved Mozart,
and Wallace Stevens, who did not—

I listen on my earphones to a Mozart piano concerto,
and as his melodies
reach me again like the nostalgia of adolescence

I remember an elementary school teacher
who taught us that Mozart's father punished him cruelly
to goad him to grow as a musician
as a boy of four or five,

and how she genuinely marveled that instead of hating
music for that
Mozart made endlessly joyous music

as a boy and an adolescent and a man,—

though I wonder if one could really tell the eras apart
in his innocent music:

the eighteenth century as a long coda,
boyhood as a colony
that never hears of the metropole.

THE DREAM OF PROPERTY

We have awakened from it.

But it shades our mood,
asks us an incomplete question.

•

Gardens
in Michigan:

our tomatoes tasted of the earth.

•

Others, many others,
are still sleeping—
outer doors locked,

inner doors open.

•

What is the most beautiful dawn
you have ever seen?

I think of a noon,
throwing a tennis ball against a brick wall
in the side yard
of my childhood home.

•

Impurity implies purity,
irrationality implies rationality,—

thus, private property
implies the commons.

JULY BALLAD

Feeling the sadness of those without an imagination—

looking out the window
of the second floor living room in a resort
at the green and brown branches of a fir—

my work is more than half done,
by any measure—

what would it feel like to live
without an imagination?—

would your heart and mind
be closer,
or more distant?

the one freedom my heart tells itself it lives with,
the way the mind draws breath—

heart and mind,
joined by an image:

what do you feel,
brown branch on a living tree?

WHITNEY LOAN

In graduate school,
at the end of one summer,
preparing to teach Coleridge to a composition class,

I drove myself from Berkeley to Mount Whitney,
four hours away,
to try to summit the tallest mountain in America.

I slept in the campground at the base of the path
and woke early the next morning to get a permit
hoping to make it to the top and back in one day,

though the recommendation is to take two days,
camping halfway up the ascent for the night.

I didn't make it—
I turned back with a severe headache from the altitude
and finished the defeated hike in the dark of evening
of my first day there.

I've been reading Heidegger on Nietzsche:

I want to understand the will,
the idea of the will to power,
why it captured me and why I now take leave of its rhetoric.

For me as a man
the will has to do with identifying with the focal fury
of a hard-on:

it is metaphysical in that way.

I don't think men talk about sexuality enough
when we are discussing philosophy,

and so this poem that begins in failure
ends at the advent of another path.

FIFTY-FIFTY

Lo mejor del paraíso
es ir contsruyéndolo.

I heard this from my wife's cousin
at the family farm
in the interior of Guatemala
about a year after we were married:

The best thing about paradise
is to be caught up in creating it.

It scared me,
in my childless late twenties:

no finish line,
no rest,
no cold beer on the porch?

But now I understand,
twenty years later.

The best thing about your life
is that it is right here,
right now—

not telling you what to do.

"BEAUTIFUL EXPERIMENTS"

I live in the town where I went to high school
thirty years ago.

I left for fourteen years,
from age eighteen to thirty-two.

It was a hero's journey:
I traveled, I found the question, I was transformed,
I found my love,
I returned to teach in my hometown.

Last fall, driving my son and his friends home at midnight
from a school drama
in our minivan,
we passed a woman who could well have been a prostitute
walking alone on Main Street.

I may have been the only one to notice her—
nobody said anything.

And what would we have said?

To leave,
there may be no more important right for a woman,
for the two women who have left me:

silent, dark caresses and tenderness, passionate burning—
somehow to share this with a woman
seemed to insinuate a promise between us,

because I am sentimental, I suppose,
which means according to the authority I've read
that my politics are deficient in hope:

for I understand love as the height of freedom,
whereas, really, struggle is the height of freedom.

TWENTY-FIRST ANNIVERSARY

—for Melanie

I think it is purely sweet,

my memory of the day we said
no falls could disunite us.

THE GOOD FIGHT

This is what my boss,
the associate dean,
said she thinks I have been doing, have been fighting,
for many years.

The good fight is a fight against cruelty,
coldness,
self-satisfied indifference.

The wagons of victims of communism,
of fascism, of neoliberal terror:

the good fight is to decide where to lead it,
not to be afraid to look back.

RESENTMENT BLUES

You spot it, you got it.
That's how my queer son looks at homophobes.

I wonder if the same is true of resentment,
a black and gray blight on nearly every green leaf
of our democracy.

In my twenties I resented those whose academic careers
took off while mine languished.

I was bitter.
And now I am not.

But I see bitterness everywhere today—
our politics are full of bitterness.

How do you heal from it?

Ressentiment:
reactionaries like Harold Bloom and Nietzsche
used the word for scaffolding
to their white summit.

I don't know how you heal from resentment,
but I did.
Good fortune alone doesn't explain it.

Maybe just to choose carefully what you resent,
so that it doesn't kill you
from the inside out.

My townspeople,
what can you resent
in the lightness of your heart?

Or perhaps that is the wrong question,
perhaps I misunderstand
and you are all shallows,
always have been—

the shouting, fervid masses at the resentful rallies
go home and dream of the ocean,

sleep and dream of their mothers
telling them of their goodness,

forever children, innocent,
protected by their God,
whom they must lose to be saved.

THE DICTATORSHIP OF THE BOURGEOISIE

Paper cuts
and paper boats.

And fear of the mailbox,
a world of sunsets in the future.

Letters as walls,
and frames as flowers in the garden.

Common prayer
and the weed of human kindness.

Above all pretending
to an open mind.

Though not quite pretending,
at the last,

the postage stamp of memory,
the shadow of a child.

ART OF MEMORY

Making Guatemalan enchiladas for my son's sixteenth birthday
tonight with my wife,

chopping boiled beets on the cutting board,
the tapping of the knife on the wood surface—

it sounds somewhat like a woodpecker on a pine,
I heard them years ago in another home—

I am reminded also of preparing dinners together
in our first shared home,

twenty-one years ago,
a converted garage in the Oakland hills.

It is love that allows me to look across the lake of years
the way a voice is carried on it by a breeze,

intonations and imaginations,
a conversation,

the unsaid
love like laughter becoming the very air that connects us.

ADVANCED PLACEMENT IN WORLD HISTORY

My younger son has wanted a better TV for gaming in his room.

He has always loved stuff—
I love that about him,
it makes me hopeful for him:
it's a good path to happiness, the way he lives it,
actually really enjoying possessions, attentively and patiently.

He came home from school yesterday saying he learned
that desire is the source of suffering:

he's studying Buddhism in the third week of World History,
sophomore year of high school.

And though he playfully says
he's happy to be a hypocrite,
he says he doesn't want to look for a new TV anymore,
he's happy moving an older one into his room.

And there it is,
the village raising us,
whether we would have it so or not.

My own Daoist view will probably not be presented
by the high school history teacher:

desire is natural,
it is older than language,
it is a mystery like a name:

it can take us a lifetime to understand it,
a little like a hypocrite
always teaching others in order to teach ourselves.

CONTRADICTIONS, II

Why do some people's hypocrisies delight me
and others ignite a blue flame of anger?

Do I unjustly believe that some people are obligated
to make sense,
while others should be free to be?

I suppose it matters to me if they suffer for others.
If their pink, clean-shaven cheeks
have always smiled beautifully for themselves.

But that does not explain it either;
I detest the contradictions of at least one very empathic
person, too.

Maybe it is all self-interest:
I loathe the hypocrisy that targets me in some way.

My oldest child loves those who do unselfconscious goodness.
I think that may be what piques me,
those who do unselfconscious ill—

which we all do,
their hypocrisy reminds me, too.

BOOK OF HOURS

Early Evening

Sitting in meditation past desire,
as I sometimes find my way to, for a matter of minutes,
the great peace of early evening—

if we are riven by human history,—
each of us, needing to heal, each of us blood-callous—
what is our history riven by?

by matter—
and matter is riven by the big bang:

to go past civilization,
billions of years past it and its furrow:

such a terrible name for it, the real source of suffering:
the big bang,

a phrase wholly devoid of poetry,
devoid of anything but capital's matter-of-fact prurience:

let us call it something else,
something I know the beauty and fear of
from my nights of sleepless mania:

dawn,
death's dawn.

SEPTEMBER

What is writing?—
    a dream
    remembering itself at midday—

THE BEAUTIES OF AUTUMN

Neuro-aesthetics teaches
that the same parts of the brain are active
on looking at a beautiful painting
and seeing a beautiful body.

So perhaps the roots of beauty are sexual,
though when sexuality was latent in me
as a boy
I still loved beauty, quite deeply.

The beauty of the complex skin of an apple in autumn:
red and golden, brown, with a black stem
and a black navel
where the blossom died in summer.

Now autumn in Southern California has none of
Michigan's drama,
or Duesseldorf's,—
which seem from here a little like Hamlet lifting and staring
at a stage-prop skull.

I wonder who has ever found me beautiful:
and has my mortality thus caused them any suffering,—

a man who has walked in a faintly chilly,
sunny autumn afternoon
into and out of an eternity of shadows.

COMMUNITY

In my Disability Studies class,
it's clear this is what many students are looking for:

the community,
they call it.

Most writers have a solitary side.
You don't become a writer to create community.

The late Cold War ideology that shaped my college education
said the only community created by literature
is the community of hero-worship.

My students are ironic about this idea,
to their credit.

They are trying to figure out how writing creates community,
without much help from history.
I am too.

Maybe my writing creates community
in the past,
adding a new presence to the solitude of memory.

JOY AND SCIENCE

Common sense tells us
the flat world is the center of the universe.

Nietzsche says we are
like ants on a cold rock in the emptiness of space.

Nietzsche found no joy in science.
The mirror was his final horizon.

Though I do not believe,
as Einstein did, in the mind of God,

I find that my mind has traveled light years
and that my ultimate, life,

cannot become so strange
that it undoes the joy in science,

that the vastness of the vast
and what is hidden in the minute

are no less naked to this life
than the naked eye.

THE LOST FEAST

My first semester in college
I took a course called The Bible as Literature.

The professor taught us that it was the work of human hands,
that the four human voices at the opening of the Tanakh
were not the voice of God.

In this sense,
I received a good nineteenth century education.

The human is the lower limit of our minds,
a student said to me yesterday.

The mystery of the transcendent,
the mystery of the immanent:

literature,
the fathomless mystery

so much older than where I thought to begin;
I am a translator

who translates
the emptiness of the raised chalice,

suddenly satisfied
like a chorus of applause.

BLUE

A mating call,
a liar's paradox.

Staying alone
in the marina hotel
where I stayed with my wife and daughter.

This sentence is not true,
inexpressible blue.

In my twenties I embraced psychoanalysis with my heart and mind. I have a mental illness—bipolar disorder—and therapy helped me heal from the storms of decades of my inner life, an extended childhood and adolescence of devastating upheavals in mood, losses and loneliness.

Accepting my smallness, my unusual particularity, my deep desires: even feeling loved for them, lovingly heard and seen by a brilliant elder.

As a young man I was a narcissist, too: trapped in the cell of self, goaded onward by an emptiness I couldn't accept and couldn't understand. Therapy taught me to love well, that was its greatest gift—to love myself and others with heart and mind.

Since that conversion to psychoanalysis in my late twenties, I've seen poetry mostly through the prism of therapy. As a teacher and essayist, I've said endlessly that poetry is essential because it serves therapeutic ends: deeper self-knowledge, compassion for self and others, granting time and attention to emotional nuance.

Now, in my fifties, I've begun look back somewhat differently—to see where in my life poetry has done something for me therapy couldn't. Where I needed poetry alone. And at the heart of its extraordinary strength is solitude. Therapy is the art of a pair—poetry helps to redeem, to make peace with, another kind of loneliness, the one with which we are born and die.

Shortly after I began psychoanalysis, a miserable relationship of ten years ended. I was excruciatingly lonely in the aftermath of loss. I would live only for the weekly hours on the couch—the only time I felt connected, when the grip of loneliness and isolation would loosen and leave me.

Then quite suddenly I fell deeply in love with the woman who would become my wife. She lived in Guatemala at the time and I lived in Berkeley. I went to visit her, to woo her, in Guatemala, and on the evening of our first night together there, as she was sleeping, I wrote, for the first time ever, an honest love poem.

To Rivers

Salvador.
The still quiet question of her hair
underneath the elsewhere of her breath.

Far to the north,
aspens taking the hint of August in the wind.
The accident was coming to this river free.

You wanted breath.
So you made your descent to the obscure dust of this water before.
Where did it take you but another air . . .

This is what your feet have felt in the riverbed before,
the silt is not dirt, not the earth—
and from here either side is a new bank.

PRAYER TO APHRODITE

Mighty Aphrodite—
that's what Woody Allen called you in a film,

Allen who fell in love with his step-daughter.

You have been good to me,
better than I deserve,
I want to say:

I suppose you make many men think that way.
Evolution has speared us through the guts
and we try to call it pleasure.

Please don't take back all you have given me:
that's my first petition.

Let me enjoy this early evening breeze
in the heart of the city,

in the loins of time.

SILENT INTENTION

Just went to the church at eleven-thirty in the morning
for noon mass.

The main doors were locked and two men and a woman
were waiting in front of them.

I asked if they were waiting for mass,
and they said yes.

Then the older man said,
Should we get started?

And they agreed, and began to pray the rosary.

Would you like to join us,
the darker man asked me.

No, thank you,
I said.

Our prayer intentions today,
the older man said to the other two:
Steve?

Yes, Steve, they answered.

And the souls in purgatory,
the woman said.

And I decided to walk away,
feeling I had what I was looking for:

even the worst would be bearable for me.
I will be okay,
come even the worst if it may.

TRUE TRUST

I've learned that I make grammatical mistakes
in situations where it's important not to.

I've wondered about this for a while—why?

I think they are Freudian mistakes
in the most literal sense:

I want to invite Freudian interpretations of myself.
Perhaps I could even say I need to.

So does this make me untrustworthy,
trapped behind the broken mirror?

I know my son wishes
I had protected him infallibly
at times when he was growing up.

There is nothing virtuous in my inability to write perfectly,
my disability:
my undying need to write imperfectly.

So don't trust me if you mustn't.

If you love me,
trust yourself.

THE CALIFORNIA COMPROMISE

The electoral structure that may re-elect Trump
was designed centuries ago to protect slavery.

I am endlessly willing to compromise in my private life—
in public life, I am not sure.

Simply living inside the warzone we call the national border
may be compromise enough.

To be willing to compromise sounds so mature—
and there are enough grown children
in our state houses.

But once you have compromised on a matter of principle,
then can you still draw a line?

I suppose that is the question confronting me
as I consider attending a fundraiser for Jill Stein.

Heroes forget they have compromised:
Odysseus the infidel hangs his household maids.

Women know how it feels to be compromised,
almost all of them.

If you really deeply care about the feelings of someone else,
compromise is a strength, not a weakness.

Compromise is probably more difficult for men.
That, too, may be why women are drawn toward it.

We all have a chance for a moment to control the sea—
so many shrink from that, and mourn the sunlight.

JUST PROFESSOR

Martha Nussbaum says the only way to win enduring rights
for disabled people
is for institutions of education to displace the family
from the center of culture.

The first thing I think of is the residential schools
that destroyed indigenous families and lives.

And of the horrors of Soviet overreach
I heard about as a child myself.

But there may be something to this—
even my own work,
so much about family,
may be on the side of turning the family inside out.

How much can your politics and your life
be at odds?

I am a family man,
as they say at work,
and nothing is closer to me than my family.

But perhaps educators like me
should think of what we do as important
as raising a family.

Would that mean we'd work for nothing?

Perhaps only a philosopher
can be as foolish as Nussbaum.

I think of my uncle Bill
who explained at the funeral of his brother,
my uncle Garrett,
who took his own life,

that family is like a bundle of thin sticks that won't snap because of their collective strength.

That's family, he said.

That's fascism, I thought.

FORSAKEN FATHER

Seeing a video of my young nephew acting in a play
in an all-white suburb of New York,
a play attended by his parents and grandparents,

costumed like a middle-class boy of a hundred years ago.
I have been him,
trusting the script implicitly, observed by loving elders:
contented and all energy, the essential child.

Lacanians have their Freudian,
Christians have their god at least as deranged as Freud.

At a certain ultimate moment a true poet can trust,
put faith in,
only himself.

All of our systems are broken and untrustworthy,—
even my beloved Daoism,
carried only by protest into the future.

NOTHING MORE

I kept faith with the truth:
to bring light to the earth.

I wanted to be common as bread:
the fight didn't find me absent.

But here I am with that which I loved,
with the solitude I lost:—
no repose by this stone.

In my silence the sea is working.

    —my translation of "Nada Más" by Pablo Neruda

WAITING FOR LIBERATION THEOLOGY

Communists want the abolition, globally,
of economic arrangements where people profit.

I asked on Twitter years ago,
what's the difference between a communist and a cop?

A former student
from Nicaragua,
who hates America and loves poetry,
answered:

some are born cops,
and others aren't.

You can't fake it,
what you care about.

You can't fake hate,
you can't fake love.

If you would fell a tree
you would fell an orchard.

FRIDAY

Communists have no hope.
That is their secret.

Just exhausted after a week of teaching
and a disastrous election.

Music is a refuge.

I suppose I could live without hope, too.

My son rejects my Daoist belief in an afterlife
where we all return to the numinous source:

I don't want to merge with Hitler, he says.

What if you only merge with a goodness in him
he never got in touch with, I said,
that he never could express or know?

Dad, I appreciate the effort, he said,
I really do.

I'll think about it, he said.

DISAPPOINTING MARCIN

It is suspiciously easy to be anticommunist in America.
Covert manipulation and corruption of all kinds
are a tailwind,
a scepter.

Today the Democrats—like David Axelrod—
said in the news the party has become

too educated, too deferential to intelligence,
and so unable to persuade the people of its good intentions.

There is no left anymore,
a friend in her seventies said tearfully at lunch,
and the left is where literature comes from.

Perhaps this is a collage rather than a poem:

film is the genre for the illiterate,
and it does often make me resent my own intelligence.

Think:
how many centuries did it take Christianity to evolve?

It is true that we are not yet ready for communism,—
is it still evolving
in the darkness of our hearts?

THE LOYAL CURSE

My teacher looked with ironic distance
on what he called the dog-like loyalty in his nature.

I am fiercely loyal too:
but I don't especially care about loyalty in friends.

Christian fanatics
who demand it and loathe its absence are not all fools:
consider Dante.

There are concentric circles of demands
on my loyalty:

but some few things about myself
I don't feel compelled to understand,

and I suppose those are mostly
the ones I don't feel inclined to judge.

BUDDHIST INTERLUDE

To care as a teacher—
after decades,
I still care, how do I care?

There are many ways to care,
you can care for
the world of illusion—

this care is made
in the space between persons,

against that lethal peace,
nothing.

EARLY POEMS

THRENODY FOR PAUL MORPHY

An oil by my grandfather-in-law-to-be,
a saw mill owner and amateur painter
whose taste in English landscapes was transplanted
to a Mesoamerican garden by way
of Madras, rests in the light of mid-morning.
Its two figures, inexperienced in
pastoral romance, are poised on the bank of
a lake doing nothing—not even touching—
beneath a shambling sycamore, the gentle,
distant bellies of lumber-colored hills
across pale water, adrift in an idea
of the right place to fall in love so pure that
nothing even casts a shadow anywhere.
No genius or menace, just the idea that
the world changes when two people fall in love . . .

Les Fleurs du Mal festoon the baskets of a
market on the edge of town from which these two
have walked away, chess pieces and coins and glasses
of anise clinking on the sidewalk tables,
musicians not on the street but asleep in
the belfries, dogs trotting from the cemetery
to the fountain in the square and back again.

The flowers are everywhere, pungent and bright.
It could be autumn, eighteen-fifty-seven.
The tables will have filled up by late afternoon.
Chess: from Sanskrit, *chatrang*, meaning "four members,"
a florid phrase for the army. Years ago
when at night I reconstructed great games
from notations, the companionship the
chess board offers seemed ultimate and tragic—
pitiless, calculating, menacing, hard,
provisional—and among the luminaries
of its Hobbesian constellations, Paul
Morphy, a boyish Southern lawyer, grabbed my

fascinated longing like a broken
arrowhead of drifting geese. The Opera
House match against a duke and a count where he
sacrificed knight, bishop, rook and queen to win
in seventeen moves. His defeat, as a nine-
year-old, of General Winfield Scott, who spent the
evening in New Orleans on his way to
spearhead the phalanx of Lone Star
patriots towards Vera Cruz. Playing eight games
at once in the Café de la Régence, a
ten-hour exhibition, winning six and
drawing two, never removing his blindfold.

In middle age, obsessed with proving he had
been cheated of his father's fortune, scared of
being poisoned, Morphy died a bachelor in
his tub. Still his game against Louis Paulsen
in the first U.S. championship of eighteen-
fifty-seven was a life's perfection, of a sort—
the four knights' opening setting up two pawn
bunkers and a melee in the center through
which the gift of his queen sacrifice
flashed like the razorblade before the credits of
Un Chien Andalou.

I lie beneath this painting trying to finish
the last chapter of a book first laid aside
when its chronicle reached the year I was born:
crude oil crisis, night bombing of a dam in
Vietnam, mortar across Gaza and in
the Golan Heights, Chinese intellectuals
dispossessed and set to the plow, apartheid,
détente, LSD, the birth of Bangladesh.
Darkness has passed across the painted lake and
a storm has settled over the opposing
hills, soundless explosions of light bathing their

slopes and the broad field of water, isolating
the two silhouettes. Their daylit counterparts
seek shelter under an unseen sycamore
until the next remote illumination
interrupts this game of adjusting the world
with a glimpse of its indifferent expanse.
The flashes define them. They are each alone.
The plea of Morphy's play was to decreate
this isolation. Sacrifices and blindfolds—
each loss recuperated, undone,
redressed by the alluvial dazzle of thought—
the outrageous interruptions quieted,
the safety of the king hoarded in his heart.

A THROUGH G

1.

God when you disappeared the playground's sound
was polyphonic and layered and full of terror
because I could not place your own silence in it.
Suddenly, again, as in the short trimester before
your birth, none could unsay the worst.
No one else to demand of in angry fear.
Then a mother, two boys and an adolescent girl
brought you to the ticket kiosk where I stood
working to breathe and keep my darting eyes from closing.
I got lost, and you got lost, papa is what you said to me.
I held a handful of pellets you offered to the raucous goats.
I poised you on a fencepost to see the Bolivian monkeys feed.

.

2.

Today you announced you have a favorite song:
Cyndi Lauper's version of "True Colors."
Your mother and I listened to it one night while you bathed
and since then you've heard it often in the car.
And today while I prepared you to swim you watched me sing,
filling in, shyly, the muted, repeated word—*colors*.
Your bathing suit is pink and turquoise and blue.
The towel you were wrapped in is faded emerald, with a
    black tag.
The last painting we saw at the Mary Heilmann exhibit this
    afternoon
before your eyes went rose with fatigue is called
Surfing on Acid. It is beautiful, should you ever care to look:
layered bands of discordant color like strokes from an
    overgrown brush.

3.

At some point you might hear my name was in a famous book.
Over two rainy April afternoons in a Krakow flat
I met with a great poet of my lifetime and his wife,
Czeslaw and Carol Milosz. I arrived with flowers
and strawberries, my drenched shoe leather fretting loose of
    its stitches.
On the second afternoon Carol served us
slices of a strawberry tart. *Tak*—yes, okay—was the one
word of Polish I ever heard her speak. They have both died,
so mine will be the only record of those afternoons.
Carol spoke of dogwoods and John Dewey and a mutual friend.
Milosz spoke of magic, the book of psalms, and the same friend.
He had impressed us all in different ways, a lover of the
    written word.

4.

The dredge is rusted out in the inlet where we bike.
You ride behind me and sometimes tug at my shirt.
Racing teams carve past us, or bulge around us.
Across the water, kayaks for rent tally the sloping shore.
Blue herons gaze from the sedge on both sides.
Salvia and sage. Trickle and outcrop. Ripple and sky.
At the end of the path we loop to take the same way back.
Herons are flying over the dredge. Kayak paddles mill
in the still air. The wheel's shadow spins through the grass.

5.

For three weeks in the Duesseldorf maternity ward
where you were born the nurses called me *Rios*—
    your mother's name.
Twice a day we listened to your heart for half
an hour. I lectured on Melville and Hawthorne
and Sigmund Freud to a precious handful of students
in an enormous semi-circular hall, assembling furniture
in our flat late into the night. Sunsets were a blessing.
Pedaling home uphill, I sometimes thought I heard your own
being in my ears. A tall block of the Berlin Wall stands
in the center of a quad where I now teach, where you
have gone springing over a green hill to the library
and scattered *Odas Elementales* across the second floor.

6.

And this California college was founded in 1861 by pacifists.
My best student writes poems in which bombs explode.
For twenty years, every third household in our quiet
     neighborhood
depended on an aerospace firm.
The year before you arrived an African won the Nobel Prize
for a tale about a patrician judge who cannot
protect his townspeople from the bellicose
errors of their empire. He pursues a futile love affair.
(You once blotted spilled wine with a paper about this book.)
Which harm is right to refuse to do? What enterprises
are so shortsighted they should be ended? And, then, by whom?
Is there a best commandment? A second name for peace?

7.

At your parents' wedding a dozen bodyguards
stood in the July heat outside the whitewashed church.
A liberation theologian was the officiant;
many attendees were followers of the Opus Dei.
In a yellow chasuble, the father walked the whole nave twice
to celebrate the kiss of peace.
This was in your other country. Where you have had no home.
A country with twenty-two indigenous languages.
Of temples buried under easy earth.
Ten hours of driving along a two-lane road
have transported you from one coast to the other:
bird-haunted sesame plots off the Pacific; yacht harbors of
    the north.

8.

This is how I eat fish you told my mother and sister and me
one evening at our table. (Which your mother says
looks like it was stolen from an alpine lodge.)
I think you learned to talk that way from a video you watch
at breakfast while we get ready for work.
But I am not sure. There are many sources of your English now.
Maybe it was a conversation between your grandma
and her gardener. Perhaps you overheard me read aloud.
I can carry you easily in one arm—which you often ask me
    to do—
but our conversations now are more like when
your mother and I each held you by the hand and swung you,
gently, without a thought of letting go.

EARLY MAY

Every year the jacarandas begin to blossom
Right around the anniversary of my birth.

When my grandmother came to visit us in my boyhood
She walked past the cemetery and the freeway
To mass every morning at dawn.

My daughter told my wife and me,
"I know you don't believe in God—
But I do."

I cannot even join Pascal in his wager;
I am too much in love with sincerity.

I have been in hell,
When I was delusional the last time,
Convinced that a glass of water my mother offered me
Was either poison or antidote.
I had a short time to choose.
I knew I was in hell.

Now I am sane again,
But even falling asleep the night before last
I believed in hell for a moment,
A dark, infinite space without love.

The unknown future, that waits for all of us—
The brief spring of the barren jacaranda,

The faith of my son running past them to school.

BRIAN GLASER is the author of six books of poetry and many essays on poetry and poetics. He lives in Santa Ana, California, and teaches art and history at Chapman University.

• sites.chapman.edu/bglaser

www.ingramcontent.com/pod-product-compliance
Lightning Source LLC
Chambersburg PA
CBHW022037090426
42741CB00007B/1104